RESOLUTIONS TO EVERYDAY

PROBLEMS

AND MAKING LIFE WORK

Vera Key

RESOLUTIONS TO EVERYDAY PROBLEMS
AND MAKING LIFE WORK

Copyright@ 2024 Vera Key

ISBN: 978-1-956884-35-7

Contributing editors or all services completed

by Imprint Productions Inc.

Printed in the United States of America

Published by Imprint Productions Inc.

Contact
imprintproductionsinc@gmail.com / (678) 860 – 6237

For You, A Guide

This isn't just a self-help book,
It's a map I made for you.
Read it, do the work within,
And happiness will shine through.

Don't rush, take it slow,
One step, then the next.
This journey is about growth,
Not speed, so don't get vexed.

You have the power to change,
To rewrite your own story.
The past is gone, the future's yours,
Embrace your inner glory.

Commit to this work,
And watch yourself bloom.
You'll rise above past mistakes,
Leaving behind all gloom.

So, open these pages,
And let the journey start.
A brand new you awaits,
With a joyful, open heart.

The world will see you shine,
As you conquer every test.
But the greatest reward of all,
Is the peace within your every breath.

ACKNOWLEDGMENTS

I'd like to begin by acknowledging God, the source of all inspiration and guidance. My gratitude extends to my parents, whose love and support have always been a beacon in my life. A special acknowledgment goes to my beloved sister Louise, a constant source of encouragement and spiritual companionship.

My father, a dedicated minister and skilled craftsman, instilled in me a deep respect for both spiritual and practical pursuits. My mother, a wise and compassionate woman, offered unwavering guidance to all who sought her counsel. Their influence shaped my understanding of the world and my role within it.

Louise, with her many connections to her spiritual community, opened my eyes to new and different expressions. These experiences deepened my interest and dealing with others on a spiritual basis.

Our home was a temporary stop for all people who needed some relief from their conditions, whether it was for food, work, shelter, money, or advice of some kind. My Mother was always available for people. Biblical discussions and accounts of health struggles captivated my attention, fueling my desire to help others navigate both spiritual and physical challenges. I am deeply grateful to Dr. Brunetta Nelson and her exceptional team for their tireless efforts in bringing this publication to fruition. Their unwavering support and expertise have been invaluable. As always, I express my heartfelt gratitude to my students, clients, spiritual children, family, and friends. Your presence in my life is a constant source of gratitude and joy.

Finally, I extend my appreciation to everyone whose names are not mentioned here, but your kindness, contributions, and presence with me will always be remembered. Thank you so very much.

DEDICATION

This book is dedicated to all those who have, or have yet to, discover the profound truth that "we are all here to learn life lessons and to settle Karmic debts."

It is also dedicated to my family, friends, students, and clients who have embraced the processes outlined herein and, as a result, have become healthier, happier, more prosperous, and more self-aware.

My deepest gratitude goes to Pfelton, Stephenie, and Ian (my children), and to my spiritual daughters Johanna Castillo, Malaika Adero, Tyna Price, Janice English, Valerie R., Olivia G., Ellen L., and Monica M.

PREFACE - INTRODUCTION

I have always wanted to be helpful to people as early as age five. At seven years old I went to the store for the elderly in the neighborhood and assisted them in any way I could. I mainly ran errands for them. As I continued to grow, I always wanted to help them with the health conditions they shared with my mother. Rheumatism, arthritis, and minor aches and pains. Their conditions were few back then, but common to them. I used to wish I had a magic wand that I could wave, and they would be healed immediately. So, health and healing have always been a part of my interest in people.

After going to college for a year, I decided to go into the medical field. I became a professional nurse. I worked in the operating room for one year and realized that I never saw the patients after we had repaired or removed the defective parts or problems they had. I decided to become a nurse in 1970. I took the international state board exam for nurses and passed with flying colors! I worked in all areas of the healthcare field that I desired. One day when I was doing home care with a patient, I noticed that the medication wasn't helping her anymore and she was still in pain.

I then decided that there were alternatives that could be taken. I had heard from other people that some patients had gone out of the country for their healing. I wanted to know Why. I have had a lot of spiritual experiences in life, in my childhood, and continuously as an adult. I always wanted to play school when I was a little kid, and I had to be the teacher.

The females back then always wanted to play house, but I won most of the time by suggesting to them to play school first.

I decided to go to a class at my Church in May 1972. The class was about the interpretation of one of the books of the Bible. I was sitting in the front seat dozing through the whole hour, on and off. Each time the instructor asked a question, I answered correctly. He just laughed and noticed that I was dozing in the class.

Anyway, I got to the idea that I would teach metaphysics for seven weeks on Sundays from 6 PM to 7:30 PM. I invited eight clients to get them prepared for the next course at the church. I took out my contact book and called each person to inform them of the seven-week class. They all agreed and came on time.

On the seventh Sunday after the class, I made the announcement and told them that they were now ready for the next course at the church. Martha stood up and said, "She did not want to go to another group or class. She asked why I could continue facilitating the class. I did not have an excuse or read on. I continue to teach classes for 21 years at my home. All of their family and friends wanted to join and they saw the difference in the way that each one of them lived happier, healthier, and prosperous. I was doing my meditation and afterward, it came to me very clearly to write the *"Resolutions To Everyday Problems"* book. I called seven people that I had been counseling and invited them to attend my *"Resolutions To Everyday Problems"* class. I had planned to teach it for seven weeks on Sundays for one and a half hours. They all came and were as excited as I was. I didn't teach from a book or notes when I started the course, I just taught it the way the Spirit gave me the information. The classes were so impactful that the students started asking if they could bring their family and friends too. The results the participants received were so pronounced that their family members and friends wanted to know what had caused them to be renewed in joy, prosperity, and health!

Others got involved in the course and I had to expand the space. For 21 years, every Tuesday and Sunday, I taught the classes straight through before taking a short break.

The classes went from spiritual development, effective prayer, and dream interpretation and now **Resolutions** *to Everyday Problems.* People from all walks of life came and received it. It was two of my friends who kept asking
me to write a book. The two in particular were Pat Daly and Lavada Collins. I just didn't take the time to write books back then. I already had a lot to do. So, after dealing with family life, working in the medical field, teaching, counseling, hobbies, and visiting family, and friends all over the states; I have finally decided it's time to complete and publish this book. I've taught it for years, and now it's in print.

Writing is embedded in my life; I've been writing since I was four years old. I did my oldest sibling Mozella's homework while she was in the first grade through the fourth grade. I would pretend that I was going to school too! So, my skills for entertaining my mom were to tell her the poems and stories I made up. In August 2008 a very dear client of mine asked me to write a book. I supported and shared with her some processes through a difficult challenging pregnancy. And, of course, the processes from this book worked! About a year later, she told her friend who had very similar issues how I helped her. She told her friend to do exactly what I had told her to do. A few days later her friend called her and told her how everything had worked out perfectly for her too. Her friend used the instructions just the way she had said. That's when the urgency and call to write the book, ***Resolutions to Everyday Problems*** Before she called, I was in North Carolina with a friend of mine, and I had just gotten the message from my meditation that I would write another book. So, when I got the telephone call, I already knew the topics I would write about just like I did when I taught the first class in 1972. So, between doing TV programs, traveling to different states doing programs, workshops and seminars, interviews, and so forth, I served private clients and attended to my family. The book is finally, here, continue to enjoy and be transformed! Is this the name of a book?

The book you are about to read is like a journey you will be going on. The hardest Truth to accept is that your life's events are yours to repair, resolve, and recreate! When things don't go the way you like them; like them the way they are. Choose an emotional response that you have learned or a pattern you've used that no longer serves you and can be changed, only by you! To accept the fact that this is your world and all that happens in it is for your own highest good in one way or the other, is your best. You get a lesson or a blessing. And the lesson is the blessing. So, choose to move forward and break old habit patterns.

The adage" old habits die hard" is true, and old patterns die harder! You will find out what the popular patterns are, how you got them, what they do in your life and body, and how to resolve them! You will also learn how to handle your emotional upsets in a manner that works for you and all you are in contact with. You will resolve issues that have plagued you for years. You will see how misperceptions and misinterpretations of some events in your life have caused you to go in circles in your life and still not be content or happy!

You'll discover how old pinned-up anger at someone can block the way you receive your substance in life. When you realize that the things that have happened in your life and the inherited patterns that you've picked up are not your lot in life, you will be able to see how these events have been part of the reason or all of the reason why you are the way you are! If you are satisfied with that, okay. But if for some reason you are not, then you should seek to change the pattern. You will find out that your worst enemy is not who you think it is! You'll discover that the things you thought you were doing were hurting someone else may not be that way at all. You'll learn how to forgive people who have wronged you and how to receive forgiveness from them, whether they are on the planet or not! Learn how to be forgiven and to forgive yourself as well, and much much more.

—Vera K

Table of Contents

CHAPTER 1 - WHAT ARE EVERYDAY PROBLEMS

What are everyday problems? Everyday problem refers to your unresolved issues, mental, emotional, and physical, that you deal with daily. Some of these issues started long before they show up in the body as troublesome problems. They can be traced as far back as one can remember and even in the womb. The subjective mind records everything you've ever felt, tasted, touched, smelled, or seen, which is locked away in a vault. this part of the mind does not discriminate nor choose, it merely records. This is one of the reasons a hypnotist can have a person say and do things they may not consciously say or do via suggestion.

The objective mind is that part that is conscious and makes instant connections at times the person chooses. Sometimes it is done so quickly that it may seem that they are one. take this for instance: if someone asks you your name, it may appear as an automatic response. when at some other time to recall the name of your first-grade teacher may take longer for the recall to come forth consciously! The unconscious subjective mind takes orders from the objective (conscious) mind. The superconscious mind is the higher spiritual mind that brings forth the seeming miraculous -formation that seems to baffle many. This is where creativity for art, music, revelations, and other out-of-the-ordinary info comes from. All this is to say that all kinds of memories stored in the subjective mind give you the same patterns and responses that were stored long ago, consciously or unconsciously!

Problem: You haven't spoken to your parents for years and don't intend to. They did or did not do what you thought they should have and that's too bad for them! They never bought you the pony you asked for and now they're done! Or whatever it was!

Ronnie is a construction worker. He builds houses and works outdoors; mostly he grew up around his other two siblings which are brothers Charlie and Jack. His mother was the disciplinarian of the family. And Ronnie hated that. His Dad was on the road all the time as an insurance adjuster so pretty much his mom raised all of them. Ronnie got into lots of trouble at home growing up and he stayed out after his curfew. He fussed when he had to go to bed. And he also used profanity around his friends and other kids that he played with outside.

When Ronnie was nine and 10 years old, his mom always got on his case about his attitude; and he got punished for doing wrong things. Ronnie had an attitude toward two siblings and acted angry toward them all the time. Ronnie treated strangers better than he did his family. When Ronnie wanted to get back at his parents he would deliberately do a half-done job on his chores and he would have to keep doing them over and over until he got it right! His Dad sent him to the store for a specific brand of bread and he deliberately bought the wrong brand. His Dad made him take it back to the store and get the bread he asked for.

As soon as Ronnie got old enough (21) to live on his own, he did. He got a good job and moved into his own home. Remember he grew up spending a lot of time with the boys. He got along very well with them. He pretty much got along with his dad when he was at home. Ronnie would play basketball, bowl, and other male sports with the guys after work every day. When he was around girls, he acted a little bit shy.

He was always polite around other females and their mothers. Ronnie finally married when he was 25 years old. Louise was 2 years younger than Ronnie and they ended up having 2 girls. Now the Patterns Begin! Remember Ronnie got along better with guys than girls, and now he lives around them again! Their same issues started showing up after his second daughter was born. The first daughter was 4 years older than the younger one.

Louise would now and then remind Ronnie of his mother when she had to discipline the girls. He would scold Louise in his annoying angry voice tone! She responded by shutting down and not talking, just like she had growing up at home! Louise was not Ronnie's Mom but because she was a mom too, it reactivated the old unresolved issues that he had experienced at home many years ago! This is what happens. Ronnie spoke to Louise in such a manner that one of her friends asked How could she live with that? "He always spoke in a firm harsh-like tone all the time". That's what Louise told her girlfriend. Ronnie developed ulcers at some part of their marriage. And Louise developed high blood pressure as well.
They both carried their anger and unresolved issues with their parents for many years and that's just one of their health conditions! Publicly they got along very well. They seemed to get along well and stayed married for over 45 years! So, to be happier and healthier it's best to let go of your unresolved issues!

Solution: You must find a way to forgive your parents; and now that you're on your own, you take the trip yourself! If you don't hurry and find a way to forgive them your life still doesn't work!

To harbor anger, hurt, resentment, or any other negative emotion keeps you bound to the very person(s) you'd like to be free of! Some of them are merely raising you the way their parents raised them. Doesn't work for every generation. Remember whose life is still not Working!

They did not deliberately set out to harm, hurt, or injure you in any way. They did the best they could with what they had! Get some facts about how they're doing and see if cutting them off has caused them any problems. They could be doing the same old things they did before, and you are still suffering! Read the emotions section and work on the resolution.

Problem: Expectations can almost guarantee that you've set yourself up for disappointment; they are anticipated results that will turn out in a particular way, according to your plan.

You have a guest list set and RSVPs attending, all but 3 show up! When others are involved in your setup (expectation) you may or may not get the intended results. When someone has to be, act, or respond to you in an anticipated way, it is more often than not, a form of control! You could easily be trying to make yourself comfortable! Read the section on control manipulation.

Staphenie is a 31-year-old Administrative Secretary. She applied for a job at a Corporate America Company position that was looking for an employee to replace the one that had left their office. Staphenie had 3 years of experience in this position and had been called in for an interview. She was professionally dressed as always and was interviewed by a manager that she would be working under.

The interview went very well and Staphenie had done an excellent job answering the manager's questions. She was then introduced to a second manager and was interviewed by that person too. And yes you got it, Staphenie impressed that manager as well. The interviews lasted for more than an hour! Staphenie left with high expectations that she would be starting that new job very soon. She waited patiently for 2 days, no call. Then three more days and no call again. After a week went by, She gave up on that job and dealt with her disappointment. She decided that there must be a better position for her somewhere else.

She never got a return call from that company! She moved on to her next interview with another company that hired her on the spot and she stayed with them for eight years until the company moved out of state! Expectation, disappointment, and resolution. Staphenie was told to apply elsewhere for a job, forget the disappointment, and keep her work search continuous. She had to keep in mind that there was a better position waiting for her. And it was!

Mary is a mother of three, two girls and one boy. All the kids are teenagers and in high school. Tammy, the eldest of the three, is 17 years old, Callie is 15 and Bobby is 14. Mary is a single mom now because her husband's job moved to another State that she was unwilling to move to! Mary works two jobs to support the family. School is in session and it is November and Tammy goes to her Mom and admits that she is pregnant! Mary is so surprised that she shows her disappointment immediately. Then she started fussing and telling Tammy how she had expected her to be the first of her siblings to finish school, go to college, and set an example for her siblings; but now she's pregnant and school is on hold!

The choice of solutions was to go to night school later, back to day school after the birth, get her GED and go on to college, get married, and or give the baby up for adoption! These were the only choices Mary gave Tammy. Mary's expectations fell through. Expecting someone else to do something may or may not pan out!

Solution: Accept it the way it is, knowing that whoever is there is supposed to be. Make the proper adjustments and enjoy the ones that did come!

Problem: You stop speaking to your Mom or Dad for years, you also disagree with a family member, and you refuse to communicate completely. You cut them out of your life for good and never to speak again!
Jeanette is 29 years old; she went to high school in her birth town, which is Arizona. She left after graduation and went to college in New York, never to return. She would not call her Mom or Dad and neither go visit them. After she left over ten years ago; she was still angry with them because she wanted a pony, and they never bought her one. She wanted to go to Washington DC to see the Statue of Liberty from age 5, every year until she was 12 years old. She got mad about it. She did her work, became quiet, and stayed to herself. She decided that no matter what her parents gave her she'd never forgive them.
Years have passed and when I met Jeanette there was a second issue. She was wondering why her relationships had not worked and why the guys always left her. The female friends don't hang around long either!

My first question to Jeanette was if she wanted to keep the anger she was carrying toward her parents. She said "Yes". I then asked her if her parents raised her from birth. She said they did. Then I proceeded to give her the resolution. I reminded her that her parents were adults before she was born. And when she does not come home or call them, they know that she is upset or angry. They do not like it, but they've accepted it because that's how she has been acting. I told her that the anger was causing her to be devitalizing her body's health. She is unhappy and unforgiving to her parents. I told her that her parents are the fundamental relationship. And that her anger wasn't hurting them, only her! When there is an upset with the Dad, life doesn't work with the males in your life. If the upset is with your Mom, you'll have problems with females. So pretty soon she would have headaches that could turn into migraines, stomachaches that could eventually turn into ulcers, and the list goes on! Your life doesn't work when you carry old hurt, pain, resentment, or anger. Parents usually are trying to do the best that they know how under the circumstances. They are not trying to deliberately set out to harm or hurt you! Your life and relationships are not working because of a lot of unresolved issues with your parents. I then told her that she would have to forgive them before her life works. The forgiveness process works right away!

Solution: Notice whether you are withholding yourself due to fear, anger, resentment, or control. Check your pattern to see if this is how you've always handled things when you had a disagreement with them or someone else. Be willing to resolve the issue rather than avoid the person or just vent. There are a few ways it can be handled so you will still be okay, peaceful, and content. Read the section in the book on Forgiveness and Anger.

Problem: Criticizing others negatively, did you know that criticizing someone means that you're dissatisfied with yourself? This means Self-dissatisfaction and seeing clearer in the person being criticized by them. "Judge not, that ye be not judged".

When Donald turned twelve years old, he had to go to the doctor. He had an infection in in left foot and had to soak it for one week in an antibiotic solution. His little sister, Jackie, seven years old, saw him in pain, frowning. She asked him if there was anything she could bring him, a glass of water or some milk and cookies. He got angry and hostile and yelled at her and told her to leave him alone and not to come around him! Donald's sister was only trying to help him, but that anger was still there. He only acted angry at home toward his family, *all females*. As they continued to grow up Donald and his sisters didn't get to see their father very often. He had moved out of town!

NOTES

CHAPTER 2 – RELATIONSHIP ISSUES

One day Henry eased into the room at the time his older sister, Janice, and their cousin were looking at the Miss America Pageant. They were both eighteen. They were criticizing every person who came out on stage. They talked about how they looked, how they were dressed, their hairstyle, and how they appeared to them. All negative statements! Some of the things the girls were saying they had been told to them by their relatives or friends. When they were growing up, they were dissatisfied with how they dressed and looked! So, each time they got a chance to criticize and judge someone else, that is what they did! If the girls had looked inside themselves first, before criticizing the pageant girls, probably wouldn't have been that descriptive of them! All of his family members acted nice and polite in public. It was just when they were comfortable at home that they acted the way they felt.

Henry is now 21 years old. His mom and dad were married for fourteen years. When he turned eight years old his parents got divorced and Henry rarely saw his dad, very little after that. The next time Henry saw his dad he was twelve, the short time he spent with him, his dad claimed Henry's mom was the reason why he didn't see him more often.

That wasn't the truth. For years, Henry grew up angry at his mom for not letting him spend time with his dad. He grew up angry and rebellious against his mom and two sisters. When he was 15, he was out with his friends on the basketball floor in the gym, when a pretty girl noticed the guys playing, he would claim the girl was a nerd or too expensive to invite out! Criticizing and judging continued to grow, and he became eighteen. He then had a steady girlfriend, but the relationship did not last very long. All the dates that he had were short. All of them ended up with the girls having to end their relationship with him because he was angry, or he acted out at some point that was embarrassing to them.

Henry continued to have issues with all the girls he met! His relationships with females do not work! He claims he tries very hard, but the girls are not right! He always blamed the girls in the relationship. Without being aware that the girls he met were all different; he was the same! But he always blamed them saying that it was their fault for some reason or another. Henry is at a stage in his life where his anger with his mom and sisters has caused him to not have good relationships with females at all; he criticizes them, judges them, and ends up being alone!

What Henry needs to do now is to realize and take responsibility for his angry attitude toward women in general. He should write a letter of forgiveness to his mother, his sisters, and any other females that he's criticized and blamed. And a letter of forgiveness to himself for carrying this upset for all of these years! This way he can clear his relationship issues with girls and be free of his own choice to be angry with females! Now his relationships work.

Solution: The next time you get tempted to criticize someone, stop and dig deep within yourself for the same quality or character trait that is unfavorable inside you! The other person is only reflecting it to you more clearly; when you go within and process your issue it will not bother you at all. You can always clear your issues, not theirs! Read and work with the Ultimate Truth process.

Problem: An event or situation is not going the way you want it to. No one is cooperating. Disagreements, resistance, arguments, and so forth are happening. The problem is who's taking care of Mom? Mrs. Nichols has eight children, all of them are adults now, the oldest daughter lives out of state and the others all live in the state where Mama Nichols lived. She got sick and all the kids got together to decide who was going to take care of her when she came home from the hospital.

Knowing all of the information out of three men and five women they all had the meeting. All of the children were married and had their own families and own homes for many years. The youngest of the females was the only one who had been divorced. She had three children and was a professional nurse. The ages of the family members were from ages 56 down to 35.

The disagreements started when one wanted to do one thing, and another wanted to do something else that was not in sync with everybody else. The youngest daughter thought that the meeting would go well because all of the older siblings would be able to run things. The youngest sister's expectations didn't happen. She accepted the arguments and disagreements for over 20 minutes! She had to take over and tell them exactly what needed to be done first! More important than the house stuff! They all wanted to take care of the house, and the yard, one wanted to take care of the bills, one wanted to take care of the rooms being repainted, etc., everything except taking care of their mother. Who is going to take care of mom? She put the meeting back on track.

Solution: Look and see that you're trying to control it and when you do, you'll have to first accept it the way it is, and then you can change it! Trying to control others can be burdensome and frustrating.

NOTES

CHAPTER 3 - FAMILY

Who do you know that has the perfect family? I mean they have no complaints about the members at all! Whatever your definition of a perfect family is, it may be different than what you have. As children grow up, they have an idea and a few plans of what they think perfect families are supposed to be about.

They think about the money that they should have or that they should be able to do things and go places. They look at other families and other people and compare their families based on what they see. They think that's why I said that if they want a perfect family, they should create it themselves when they get married and have children. They will learn that the family structure is not always easy, it's not what you see, and it doesn't always work the way they see it or set their minds to believe. Life lessons and karmic debts are for all of us, period! Some of them get into trouble. They have health conditions; they break all sorts of rules and laws. Truth is, there is no way one can accomplish this feat. The very best way to deal with this is to work with what you have to make it better, and or accept the one you have already. The way they are and are not! Then, at a later time in your growth, with lots of luck, experience, and maturity, you may be in the space of being the example of the kind of family you'd like to have had! Create your own family according to your definition. Remember what is, Is, and what isn't, Isn't. Remember to see if what you want as a family is realistic or whimsical! Look at the word family, it means people living together usually with common ancestry; a group of people all living in the same household.

You may ask yourself what's familiar about you and your family. If you grew up around your biological Mom and Dad, check out the character traits you have in common with them. Better still check out the qualities your other siblings have in common with them as well. Usually, families have a position set for each child. Of course, this doesn't apply to all but take the typical ones.

Very often the eldest child has a position of being in charge, setting an example for their younger siblings. They are sometimes the protectors of the younger and in some instances the second parent. They are expected to be more responsible and dutiful. You have heard of the horror stories that the younger children have told about the older ones taunting them. Strangely enough, the little kids don't forget! There are family patterns that you picked up when you were growing up all along. If they were ones you considered good ones, keep them. The others that were not, you should have abandoned them long ago. You didn't and now you respond just the way you learned it.

Now that you know that your families are the people you had your first experiences of life with and that you don't have to keep the same old patterns that did not work and change them at the core. Some of the family members consider themselves close and spend lots of time together. If this is some trait you want to continue, you certainly can. If another feels estranged and chooses to express differently he may do so. That's what choice means. When you automatically respond in a way that no longer serves you, you are not coming from choice! That's why you are still dissatisfied. So traditional family curses or bad patterns are changeable! But only by you!

NOTES

CHAPTER 4 - DAD

Dads are very different in how they operate in the family. Most of them have a specific personal viewpoint as to how they want to appear to their mates, their children, and the world. This image they have created for themselves is usually the very reason why a lot of them die before women do! Some men are stuck with their unresolved issues, problems, and upsets because they refuse to share what their emotions are relaying to them. Their image of what a man is supposed to be like keeps them stuck! A lot of them refuse to seek help from third parties because they have unresolved issues with their Moms and or Dads.

If a female counselor is the person chosen, he has to put up this front so that he doesn't appear as a weakling. If a male is the counselor, he feels that he's just like he is and he doesn't want to appear that he is not smart enough to run his household and appear as a wimp! His attitude speaks for itself; the unresolved issues arise, and he will sabotage the session, if necessary, and may not see the counselor at all. So very often they stay stuck with emotionally unresolved issues. Long-term periods of these issues devitalize the body and cause all kinds of health conditions, which eventually lead to faster death. When there are unresolved issues with the Dad figure of the home; the person afflicted has to write a Forgiveness Letter to him, getting up and out of all of the upsets. It should be done whether the person is on the planet or not! See the section on Divine Forgiveness.

NOTES

CHAPTER 5 - MOM

Mom in the family is the receptive one. She's considered the one the kids are to cater to first. The bonding process that takes place during the gestation period brings forth some specific connections between mother and child. During the last trimester of pregnancy, it is said that the child picks up the mother's moods and feelings. I believe this happens throughout the entire pregnancy. If the child was planned and wanted, they tend to be happier growing up than the ones who were not. When the child is "trained in the way it should go; it will not depart". Straying away and departing the training is different.

If the mother has unresolved issues, incomplete(s), and depending on what's happening at the time she carries the child; the child will pick up those issues and respond to them the way she does! Whenever there are unresolved issues with the Mom figure the child will have problems with females. These problems can be traced back to the Mom! One of the ways of settling these issues is to write a Forgiveness Letter to the Mom.

The child must write down the event(s) in as much detail as possible. See the section on Divine Forgiveness. Moms are the nurturers in the family. She teaches the child love and how to care for themselves and others. She promotes the growth, development, and progress of the child. Honor thy mother and thy father so that thy days may be long upon the earth, are seen in children very clearly. The behavior, self-respect, and manners are usually intact. Their values are clear to them, and they are pleasant to be around.

NOTES

CHAPTER 6 - CHILD

When a child is being raised properly the child knows that he doesn't have to have everything he wants; especially when he's a toddler and up in age to 10-12 years old. He also knows that he is a child and is dependent on his caretaker(s) to know what to do. Some parents err by giving the child everything he asks for and or everything they didn't get when they were children. Big mistake! The child will get to the point where he knows the parent either doesn't know what to do or doesn't care about him at all; (the child's interpretation). They also grow up distrusting their parents and may look to their friends or others they feel know more. They are subject to feeling anger toward their parents.

Children are good judges of character and are quite apt in discerning the emotions of adults! They understand things first. Although they may not have the terminology nor the jaw muscle development to say what they feel or know it still doesn't negate the fact that their understanding is intact. That's why when the parent tells the child "NO" or "Stop" the child responds. The very best a parent can give to a growing child is LOVE, of course, and the encouragement of faith in the child himself. The parent should instill self-confidence in him and prepare him for dealing with the world through his independence! Another big mistake the parents make is to try living their lives through the child. You will have a far happier child when he is allowed to choose his career in life within reason! If he has been trained/raised in such a way to have faith in himself, he will be successful.

Some children today are so angry for reasons they do not know. A lot of them were born with this anger due to the mom having lots of personal unresolved anger herself. The mom may even be too young and environmental conditions during the pregnancy were not satisfying. Some of the children have this anger, again because they feel unloved by the parent(s), they get shipped off to nurseries where strangers raise them and they may feel that maybe they were not wanted!

The child has a way of checking out who in the caretaker club has the most authority (power), the mom or the dad. This is one of the reasons why agreement, communication, cooperation, and compromise are so important in the family. Some children (adults now) blame their parents for how they turned out. They forget that they have freedom of choice now and don't have to keep the dissatisfying patterns going. Choice has always been the major key. Children growing up in a large family tend to make choices about their lives a lot earlier than the smaller group. They choose patterns of the Mom, the Dad, or something different, sometimes opposite. And end up expressing exactly like the parents anyway in pattern. This is where knowing how to forgive and let go of the past comes in. Check to see if you are still operating from patterns in your environment that don't work.

NOTES

CHAPTER 7- EMOTIONS

An emotion is a mental energy set in motion through feelings; any of them love, joy, fear, pain, etc. It's a subjective response to something or someone. In a well-balanced person, emotion is controlled by the intellect, but in others, there is conflict between the emotions and the intellect. Uncontrolled emotions produce all kinds of chaos; unexpressed, they produce confusion, conflict, and complexes; for energy will have an outlet. Bottled up, it creates pressure that is the cause of much damage to the physical body. Usually, when someone refers to a person as being emotional, it often means the person is very sensitive, and their feelings are fragile. The real truth about emotional people is that they are expressive with their emotions; no matter what they're feeling, joy, peace, happiness, anger, hurt, pain, and so forth. Therefore, unresolved emotional upsets don't work.

Emotional shut-down occurs when someone has had a traumatic experience and will not allow emotional expression. The sympathetic nervous system does this automatically in the body but will gradually let the emotions return to expression.

When a person shuts their emotions down deliberately for some time they will allow themselves expression later in a twenty-four hour day. This particular shut-down is not fear-based; it's usually for temporary personal emotional protection. On the other hand, fear-based emotional shutdowns are almost always connected to some uncontrollable event. This causes more damage to the physical and mental body of the person. Again, devitalizing and damaging it in many ways with conditions internal and external as well.

Take these examples below: when some people bottle up their emotions, they are subject to inner health conditions. High blood pressure, stomach ulcers, headaches, depression, stroke and so the list goes on. The physical body suffers greatly. When a person is balanced, they can choose intellectually how they will and when they will express their emotions appropriately. They are usually calm and poised and can handle the condition with tact and diplomacy. Sometimes doctors and nurses shut down their emotions to handle their jobs, especially in emergencies. When they are not emotional in a task or treatment, they are more effective.

Imagine a doctor listening to different patients complaining of their different health conditions constantly. If he or she got emotionally involved they would be basket cases themselves and therefore unable to assist their patients! A person who displays confusion may have all kinds of made-up thoughts and viewpoints about something or someone, even themselves.

NOTES

CHAPTER 8 - EMOTIONAL SHUT DOWN

Everybody and anyone who has ever gone to a doctor knows that they are notorious for emotional shutdown. When the patient comes in and starts complaining about all his health conditions, how bad they are feeling, where all the pain is, and so forth. The doctor automatically says let's get this taken care of and see what's going on. And we'll go from there. He probably emotionally shut down properly. Can you imagine how that doctor would feel by the end of the day if he listened to all of his patients moaning and groaning? He shuts down emotionally so that he can handle all of the conditions and the health problems that come in that day. The doctor would be a basket case himself if he had to listen to all of his patients regularly every day! EMTs and other medical professionals have to shut down emotionally to handle situations so that they can do what needs to be done to save the patient!

When someone shuts down it's the act of cutting the other person off. That other person feels alone although in body the shutdown party is present! This is intentional by the person who shut down, it can be a habit and the individual uses this technique to control and manipulate. Each time this occurs the communication lines are broken. Carried too far and too long always ends the relationship. The other person or persons feel disconnected and rejected and will eventually go away.

The party who has shut down ends up being stuck with all the unresolved thoughts and feelings he had before plus, the ones he had to make up while staying shut down. Shut-down can be carried to adulthood by the child because it worked at the time, place, and with the person they grew up around. The habit has long been a pattern for them and only conscious commitment can dissolve it.

NOTES

CHAPTER 9 - DEALING WITH ANGER

Anger is an emotion that can be destructive. It can be expressed constructively if handled appropriately. Anger speeds the heart rate and pumps excess adrenaline and other chemicals through the body system. The blood pressure rises, blood flow quickens, and the muscles tense up. The whole body moves into high gear. This action can be affirmative or negative. An adrenalin rush is to take action of some kind. There are lots of ways to use this energy constructively. When anger is inappropriately expressed it can cause one to get into serious trouble.

Sandy lives with her male friend Bobby. She is 30 years old and has been on her own since she graduated from college. When I saw her for the first time I asked her a few things about her family life. And she told me that she was angry with her mom and dad. She said that she was mad at all her family members. She was very adamant about it.

I asked if she wanted to keep that anger or get rid of it. She said she wanted to keep the anger. I then told her exactly what it would do to her as far as her body was concerned. I told her that her parents already knew that she was not coming home or calling them regularly because she was angry. Therefore, they did not like it, but they accepted it because they knew how she was. I then told her that what she was doing was hurting her more than them and she was devitalizing her own body. She was having headaches and stomachaches and if she carried those for long periods, they would turn into migraine headaches and/ or ulcers in the stomach. I asked her again if she wanted to continue to keep the anger. She said, "No," she would like to get rid of it. And I proceeded to explain to her in detail what she had to do. It seems that Sandy had gotten angry with her parents when she was a teenager. She wanted to go to different dances and different events that they had in the neighborhood and at the school and sometimes her parents told her no. After all this time she was still angry with her parents and that was many years before.

Sandy recalled an incident when she was 11 years old. They were at the circus and the family was waiting in line for a show to start. She wanted an ice cream cone. She got two big scoops and when she went to show the ice cream cone to her mom, dad, and sister, smiling and skipping, one scoop fell on the ground, and everybody laughed. Then she got angry, felt hurt, and started crying. Sandy remembered that her best friend was having a birthday party in one of the community centers in the area when she was 13. She had forgotten to ask Mom or Dad if she could go. And when she finally asked them (at the last minute) the family had already made other plans for that day. She got upset about it and was angry again.

There were lots of times in life growing up when she got angry with her parents for one reason or another, but the anger had to go. If Sandy had gotten into bowling, track, softball, or any type of athletic sport in school she would've gotten rid of the anger in a very healthy manner, but she didn't and she was still stuck at age thirty! Anger has to be released!

Most people suppress anger very rapidly; it is one of the first emotions we learn to suppress. The fear and intensity and the results from incorrect expression can be detrimental! Unexpressed anger can cause even more damage to the body, internally and externally. When a person is angry and does not express it, he/she may cause all sorts of havoc and upset themselves. Accidents, falls, arguments, fights, and other disruptions can be the result, even death.

One of the appropriate ways to express anger is to first recognize it. Some people are not aware of their anger, and it stays hidden until they explode! Bottled-up unexpressed anger is the culprit. One can also do some of the little old-fashioned techniques that some train their children to do like, count to ten before speaking, run, jog, go to the gym and hit a punching bag, lift some weights, go bowling, get a pillow and punch it, and so on. There are many ways to handle anger.

Another way is to start all the sentences with *"I feel angry when"*. When talking to someone, owning the anger usually keeps you from any rebuttal. If you were to take the time to strip the anger apart, you'll find that you're never angry about what you think you are! It is coming from something else. Hurt and anger go hand in hand. The person gets hurt then they become angry. Think about it. Some are more comfortable expressing the hurt and others the anger! Giving your power away doesn't help you either. The other person knows he/she can't handle your issue.

Avoiding anger does not work! Remember uncontrolled anger gets you in big trouble. Learn to control your anger. There are ways. The first thing to do is to calm yourself down in some way. Be assertive and not aggressive. Speak firmly and clearly without insulting remarks. Listen to the other person and wait before you conclude. Negotiate and compromise when necessary.

Express yourself without getting physical or violent. Talk to someone about your uncontrollable anger, a friend, or a professional. Look in the process section of this book for resolutions.

NOTES

CHAPTER 10 - HANDLING YOUR ANGER

It's been said that anger is one of the most poorly handled emotions in society today. It doesn't have to be yours. Causes of anger are frustration, hurt, disappointment, harassment, and threats. The body reacts in this way: adrenalin and other chemicals pour into the bloodstream, the heart pumps faster, the blood pressure rises, the blood flow quickens, and the muscles tense.

The body shifts into high gear to take action for your advantage or disadvantage. Knowing how to recognize and express anger appropriately can help you reach goals, solve problems, and handle emergencies. Ignoring anger does not work!

If it is not handled it can lead to health problems, tension, accidents, and interpersonal problems. Uncontrolled anger can be dangerous. It may lead to crime, abuse, and more violent behavior.

• Keep your cool when expressing anger.
• Calm down before discussing issues.
• Find out what your motives are first.
• Are you trying to defeat the person or trying to solve a problem? If your motive is negative your results will be too!
• Be assertive, not aggressive.
•Express yourself firmly and clearly without insulting.
• Negotiate and compromise when necessary.
• Seek help if you don't constructively express your anger.

- Talk to a friend or professional about it.
- When you resort to name-calling and insults you'll have more anger.
- Don't avoid the issue and hide what you truly believe.
- Be straight but don't get physical or violent.
- Making accusations can make you sorry later.
- Listen to the other person before you make your conclusions.
- To sulk in silence won't handle the issue.
- So once again Communication is the KEY.

NOTES

CHAPTER 11 - DEPRESSION

What is it and where does it come from? Depression is anger turned inward. When someone is angry about something, they at some point turn the anger inward, toward themselves, instead of expressing it in other ways. Depression means low in spirit, held down, or pushed downward. This is similar to suppression or repression.

When you suppress your anger, which is to take some kind of action, one of the ways you respond is to turn it inward on yourself, and then you become depressed. Some people think that feeling depressed is bad. It's not. The bad part is when it is taken to the extreme for long periods. And that can apply to any negative emotion! So, to handle it is to first accept that it's there, acknowledge it, and then do what has to be done in your life anyway. To ignore it, and hope it goes away without acknowledgment, or hide it, pretend it's not there or some other attitude only makes you more depressed! Feelings, just are, and handling them is better than not. They usually don't just go away without some personal form of attention on your part.

The worst thing about having an issue is to not recognize that it's there at all. When this happens there is no relief for you because you can't dissolve what you don't have! So, the best way to handle something is to first recognize that you have it. Your feelings won't lie. It's one of the ways the body alerts you that something needs to be handled in the first place! So, when there is awareness of a condition, there can be healing. In "A New Earth", E. Tolle author, gives a complete detailed explanation of how a person can press their energy so much that they end up pressing the very life force out. See the chapter on *Depression,* in his book.

NOTES

CHAPTER 12 - IN CONTROL

Several years ago, I visited one of my friends who lives out of town. I was at her house sitting at the table when her brother came by to visit. When he came in, he sat down talking freely and we both laughed and talked. He decided that we were going to play a game. Teddy spoke the words and said, "I want to let you know right now I like to be in control". And I said, "What do you like to be in control of," he became totally quiet. After a whole moment of silence, I asked him again, "So who do you like to be in control of?" This time the silence was so thick; it could be cut with a knife! So, I told him to wait a minute, and I will be right back. I went and got a spool of thread and cut it about 1 foot long. And then told him to hold onto one end of the string I held on to the opposite end of the string and I told him to pull it his way and then I'll put it back my way and we pulled it back and forth back and forth he then said what does this mean? I said, "We have a tug-of-war going right now. Sometimes it's on your side and sometimes it's on my side. If you let, go of the string then the tug of war is over. So, I let go of the string. he said while smiling, "But I have the string, I won" and I replied, "So what are you going to do with it? I'm not connected anymore. You're all alone with your item!"

What do we mean about being in control? What is control? To exercise a decisive role in influencing the actions and conduct of. To control one's own emotions, exercise power over, dominate or rule, power to direct or regulate, and restrain. Self-control. Most people who love being in control are subject to the experience of all aspects. Not only do they experience the power to influence and dominate they are subject to the negative side of it also. The negative side works like this: the person that one thinks they are controlling is merely cooperating with them at that time. The moment he/she no longer wants to cooperate, then the tug-of-war begins.

There's just a push-pull sort of event that goes on. The person in control has to use more force and or power to have things their way. There's the punishment, threats, etc. This may appear to work for a short time and then back to the tug again. The in-control person is unhappy and so is his controlee! At some point, because he/she feels restrained, the controller starts to figure out ways and means to do or undermine the controller. At some point, they always do, even if they have to run away. The easiest way to deal with control is to be free of it. The only one to control is you. If self-control is exercised at all times the freedom to respond in any situation is available to you in the present time. Peace, contentment, and self-confidence stay intact.

Some people who grow up controlling their environment usually end up with major trust issues. Their home life was so unstable that they grew up distrusting others, themselves included. There was someone in this family who was sick, abusive in some way, and /or an addict. The person felt that it was necessary for their survival to only depend on themselves! Unfortunately, they carry these qualities into adulthood when they multiply into other added unresolved issues. They then further de-vitalize and damage the body and mind. You can see that there is a rigidity and stiffness about them. Being self-controlled looks like one is out of control. Self-confidence and peace are there, and the person can freely respond to whatever the situation calls for immediately. Self-control is as good as it gets. Being in control is very limiting and is usually always fear-based. Since the person doesn't trust they are usually very uncomfortable in new situations they've not experienced. True control is not fear-based at all. One of the best ways to handle being in control is to learn to trust exclamations; it can start in small installments and then become progressive. The person has to process their self-doubts and fears from the past. It may take lots of effort on the part of the individual, but it is well worth the time.

What do we mean about being "in control"? What is control? To exercise a decisive role in influencing the actions and conduct of. To control one's own emotions. Exercise power over, dominate or rule, power to direct or regulate, restraint. Self-control. Most people who love being "in control" are subject to experience all aspects of it. Not only do they experience the power to influence and dominate they are subject to the negative side of it also. The negative side works like this: the person that one thinks they're controlling is merely cooperating with them at the time. The moment he no longer wants to. The tug-o-war begins.

There's this push-pull sort of event that goes on. The person "in control" has to use more force and /or power to have things their way. There's the punishment, threats, etc. This may appear to work for a short time and then back to the tug again. The "in control" person is unhappy and so is his controlee! At some point, because he feels restrained, the controllee starts to figure out ways and means to outdo or under-mind the controller. And at some point, they always do, even if they have to run away.

The easiest way to deal with control is to be free of it. The only one to control is you. If self-control is exercised at all times the freedom to respond in any situation is available to you in the present time. Peace, contentment, and self-confidence stay intact. To overpower, dominate, rule, and regulate constraint over someone else generates negative emotional pain, discomfort, and uncertainty. Remember, the only person you can control is you. Even little kids as small as they are; are aware of "in control" events. This is not to say, don't discipline. That's a different quality altogether. "In control" is a quality that does not usually trust themselves or others. See the section on Trust.

The difference between control and "in control' is simple, control is decisive and directive even powerful. While "in control" is fear-based where distrust and uncertainty rule! Being "in control" or enjoying being "in control" is not all it's chalked up to be. When a person thinks they're "in control", the person or thing they think they're controlling chooses not to cooperate; then at that very moment, they are being controlled by them. So…are you really "in control"? Even a little toddler can play the game.

If they don't cooperate at the time, they will make sure you have a tough time putting them on a pair of sneakers. Some people who grow up controlling their environment usually end up with a major trust issue. The home life was so unstable that they grew up distrusting others, themselves included. Although not aware that they distrust themselves because there was someone in the family who was sick, abusive in some way, and or an addict. The person felt that it was necessary for their survival to only depend on themselves! Unfortunately, they carry these qualities into adulthood where they multiply into other added unresolved issues.

They then further devitalize and damage the mind and body. You can see that there's a rigidity and stiffness about them. Being self-controlled looks like one is out of control. Self-confidence and peace are there and the person can freely respond to whatever the situation calls for immediately. Self-control is as good as it gets!

Being "in control" is very limiting and is usually always fear-based. Since the person doesn't trust they are usually very uncomfortable in new situations they've not experienced. True control is not fear-based at all. One of the best ways to handle being "in control" is to learn to TRUST! It can start in small installments and then become progressive. The person has to process their self-doubts and fears from the past. It may take lots of effort on the part of the individual, but it is well worth the time! See the section on The Ultimate Truth Process.

NOTES

CHAPTER 13 – FEAR

King James Version, (KJV) says perfect love casts out all fear. Fear is the antithesis of faith. It's the negation of confidence! We find throughout the bible many references to fear; fear not little flock. The truth is fear is nothing trying to be something, and it must be handled consciously and on the subjective level as well. What does it do? It limits, restricts, immobilizes, and intensifies the person, place, or thing. The reason it's nothing trying to be something is because the thing that keeps it alive is You! Fear is a mental attitude of the mind, which can be converted into something else (faith). It is the reverse attitude of faith and is the result of the lack of faith.

Perfect Love casts out fear; that is, confidence overcomes the depression of doubt. Mental depression can produce physical and financial depression. The psychology of economic cycles proves this. Amid plenty humanity lives in want, because of fear. When we contact a larger field of faith then fear disappears. Understand that God is the Giver and sustainer of human life and expression. The being that we are is some part of the Divine. Knowing this is to overcome fear. Whether this fear is of lack, pain, sickness, or death it is always a belief that there is something else other than Life or that Life withholds Pleasure, peace, success, and heaven from us. Love alone can overcome fear because love surrenders itself to the object of its adoration.

The soul must make a complete surrender of itself to the Spirit. So "fear not little flock for it is your Father's good pleasure to give you the kingdom". God is all there is. He is substance and supply. We must learn to accept this. And if it is God's pleasure to give us the Kingdom, then it should be our privilege to accept the gift! Fear is the reason why people stay in situations that are not for their highest good; jobs, relationships, etc. So, ACCEPT YOUR GIFT NOW!

NOTES

CHAPTER 14 – LOVE

Perfect love casts out all fear. Love conquers all! God is Love. And Love brings up everything unlike Itself! When someone falls in love with another they tend to expect that everything will flow easily and smoothly. And it does for a while; if at any time something shows up that is unlike love it will come up for healing. This is where commitment, maturity, and patience come in. The key is to have good communication take place and to be aware of the condition.

The most difficulty that will be encountered is to suppress these issues and to pretend not to notice them! Resolve them! Communication is a form of love. Think about it. When kids are cut off by being sent to their rooms when they are being punished for misbehaving, they feel this disconnection. Adults feel it too when they are not responded to when they live in the same household. If a person chooses not to talk to a loved one when they feel it is necessary, the communicator feels alone and unacknowledged! The Bible says that there are two great commandments: "Love the Lord your God with all thine heart, mind and being, and two, love thy neighbor as thyself!" Did you know that love is the central flame of the universe, the very fire itself? God is Love and we are His expressed likeness and image. Love is an essence, an atmosphere that defies analysis as Life Itself does. It is that which IS and cannot be explained. It's common to all people and all animals, and evident in the response to plants for those who love them. Love reigns supreme over all!

The essence of love, while elusive, pervades everything, fires the heart, stimulates the emotions, renews the soul, and proclaims the Spirit. Only love knows love and love only knows love. Words cannot express their depths or meaning. A universal sense alone bears witness to the divine fact: God is Love, Love is God. And God is all there IS!

NOTES

CHAPTER 15 - FORGIVENESS

Forgiveness is to give up on the mistake of the one who wronged you. To excuse for or pardon for an offense. This may seem difficult to do but it is not impossible! To forgive the shortcomings of a fellow being is to understand that all have fallen short at some time in Life. And if you do not forgive you are breaking Spiritual Law, and your life doesn't work! Unforgiveness is directly connected with your money. To let go of old hurts, pain, and disappointments is the best way to make life work.

Unforgiveness also causes all sorts of physical conditions in the body. *Matthew 9:5, 6.* Being aware that one feels that he has made many mistakes in the past can feel burdensome. When a person knows that he is forgiven by pure Love the burden is lifted and healing takes place. It devitalizes the body and condemnation being great, can cause the body to be incapable of moving. Have you ever noticed how you feel after truly forgiving someone? Oftentimes there is an emotional release after it is done. It feels as though you've released the hurt and pain you withheld all that time.

Remember when the disciple asked Jesus how many times he should forgive someone? He asked seven times. Jesus said until seventy times seven. In other words, he was saying that you should continue to forgive eternally. This is a major relief from the shoulders of each person who is aware that the Universe holds nothing against him! The ones who feel that their virtues should be rewarded more than someone else will take this as not fair. It is fair because all have fallen short of their divine calling! You can't point fingers at anyone else! Think of your shortcomings first. Forgiveness is vital because it frees you from guilt, pain, resentment, and other devitalizing qualities that block your joy, peace, substance, and happiness. See the section The Forgiveness Process.

NOTES

CHAPTER 16 - HAPPINESS

Happiness is a state of well-being or enjoyment of good of any kind. The metaphysical meaning is a state of inner peace, a consciousness of the Goodness of God, and the beneficent attitude of the Universe, a realization that can come to every man. It has a definite effect on mind, body, and affairs. A state of permanent joy. It is never the will of God for any man to be unhappy. Have you been aware of the fact that we spend lots of time trying to make ourselves happy with material things only? I'm not saying that it's not okay to have them, it's just that the joy from them is only temporary. Some people have discovered that they've missed out on a lot of wonderful small joys in life because they were striving for the things! Notice how long it takes a child to get a new toy they just had to have; In a few days, the toy is in the toy box or on the shelf. Happy for a short time.

There is lots of proof today from others who have shown us that dealing with the material side of life only, doesn't bring the fulfillment they expected. They seem to grow through one disappointment after another trying to be happy with the item(s). As children, we pick up these ideas and family traditions of striving to be, do, and acquire some things in life. That's just fine if you don't attach yourself to them. When you were a kid it took very little for you to be happy. Your Dad came home from work and spent time playing with you and you were happy about that! And there were lots of other small joys that made you feel happy.

In earlier generations when kids were kids, they lived in a less complex world, so to speak, their lives were simple, they had fewer things and yet they appeared a lot happier than some kids who had more things. Was it because they had less or was it because they focused more on truly worthwhile things? Could it mean that the simple little things bring lasting happiness? Is it possible that to love and be loved is the # one joy in life? Jesus said don't lay up treasures on earth for yourself where thieves or moths can break in and steal and destroy; but lay up for yourself treasures in heaven; love, peace, happiness, joy, contentment, satisfaction, and other good things.

The material things are transient and very changeable. This year is this style and the next year it's something else. A CPU today has to be upgraded in two years and the list goes on! We live in a state of flux and that's the joy in it! So, remember to have the material things but don't allow them to become false gods.

NOTES

CHAPTER 17 - GIFTS & TALENTS

All of us are endowed with at least one talent or more. We have what it takes, in talent, to live this life successfully now. A talent is a quality that you have that takes little or no training for you to do well. It's a natural mental, creative, or artistic ability. Sometimes so natural that it can be overlooked! You get a lot of joy and pleasure out of doing it and it feels like fun, rather than a chore. Finding your gift is not as difficult as it may appear. One way to find your natural talent is to think of things you love and enjoy doing.

Make a list of these favorite things; and if there are more than ten, choose them according to their importance to you. Then from that list pick the five that are tops to you, and after doing this, select the ones that you can turn into a service. After you discover that one, check out everything you can to see what it will take for you to be compensated for it. This is what you call doing work you love and getting paid for it.

If you put your best into what you're doing you will always receive good results. And of course, if you are trying experiments, if at first you don't succeed try, try, and try again. See if you can learn from your prior mistakes. Take this as your lesson and the hardship should disappear! Remember there are no mistakes in your process; you get a lesson or a blessing. If something you're doing seems hard for you; check to see where you are resisting it, make the correction (accepting it), and go from there.

Work is something you do to express your joy in doing it! It doesn't have to be an undesirable task. Watch people who love what they do while working. Notice how happy they are. It's your attitude that makes the difference. If it's something that has to be done, do it joyfully and you will still be compensated either by someone else or the Universe!

NOTES

CHAPTER 18— TRUST

How do you trust someone or something? You just accept the person or thing just the way it presents itself. It's like taking a ride on a carousel, you don't ask any questions you just give the ticket to the conductor and find the place where you want to sit. That's trust! You don't question what can go wrong, when the machine was last checked, or any doubt of having a perfect ride. It's the same thing with trusting a person, when they tell you (or not) that they are going to take care of something for you, you feel okay and go on with your other plans. You may not even think about the issue at all anymore; simply because you trust the person to handle it.

Trust gives you a feeling of security inside. Trust means complete assurance and certitude regarding the character, ability, strength, or truth of someone or something! Marie is sixteen years old, she lives with her grandmother and she never thought to ask if there will be food on the table if the bills will be paid, if she needs to try to get a job and do anything to help out with bills and living expenses. Marie trusts her grandmother to take care of her needs, and she does! As an adult, you may decide that you need a roommate, and your roommate is going to take care of their share of the house expenses. They have been discussed and the amount agreed upon. Sometimes they come up with excuses and say they will be late paying their share. At some point, you know you can't count on your roommate to pay. And that makes you distrust them to handle things. How do you feel now? Marie is anxious, upset, and disappointed!

NOTES

CHAPTER 19 - THE BLAME GAME

Who stole the cookies out of the cookie jar? David stole the cookies out of the cookie jar. David is one of four siblings; he has a brother named Peter, one named Lee, and one named Nathan. David was sleeping at home and all the boys were there. His mother had gone to the store and bought Oreo cookies and put them in the cookie jar. Later the three boys got together and decided that they would sneak and eat the cookies. David was asleep at the time his mom bought the cookies, so he didn't know about the cookies.

They sneaked in one by one, got the cookies, and ate all of them! And when his mother came home from her meeting, she asked who ate the cookies. They all pointed to David and said he had eaten the cookies. David didn't even know what was going on to be blamed for eating the cookies. Although he had not eaten any of the cookies, he took the blame! David got the punishment of not riding his bike for one whole week! The boys were ages 10, 9, and 8, and David was 7 years old. Their Mom knew David couldn't have eaten all those cookies, so the other boys got a punishment too! They each had to do David's chores for 1 week! What's the blame all about? Who Dunn it? Blame from the dictionary's definition means: at fault with. Hold responsible for. To make adverse comments about (someone or something) openly, often publicly and with varying severity. Responsibility for misdeed or delinquency. To blame someone for how you turned out can be questionable to an extent. Susan is 18 years old and her first year in college. She has a roommate whose name is Betty and they both were

18. Susan always admired Betty because she seemed to manage money very well and dressed very nicely. She was able to manage her allowance perfectly, Betty bought tickets to games, went to the movies she liked, went shopping with her friends, and everything else she wanted. She always had the money and funds to supply it. Susan on the other hand got upset with her parents because they did not teach her how to pay bills or how to manage money. And she didn't have many friends because she and her sister were home-schooled.   The whole time she lived at home she never had to go to the grocery store to buy food, pay bills, or do anything in money management therefore she blamed her parents for not teaching her how to manage money and her social skills were not the best. Susan struggled in school for 2 years and decided she would quit and go back later. Whenever Susan saw other girls doing things she thought she should know how to do too, she would get mad at her parents! She met Harold and after 6 months of dating, they got married! Susan is old enough at the age of twenty-one to choose how she wants to deal with some skills she missed out on. She didn't talk to her parents for a long time! After 4 years she found a counselor to talk to and got the support she needed!

You blame someone, are you saying that they are responsible for an action you took, now or earlier? Or are you blaming them for an earlier time that they should've been responsible? Keep asking these kinds of questions and see what answers you get. Though you may feel justified in your accusation; you are giving your power to handle the situation to someone who probably doesn't know they have it. And this of course leaves you stuck and helpless. When you get blamed for something, how do you feel?

When you blame someone else, how do you feel? Is it that you felt like you were attacked, injured, or defamed in some way?

Emotionally responding to a slight or indignant remark causes you to have some other negative feelings, anger, resentment, and so forth. So, you will have to handle that as well. Some people feel very different under the blame game response; some feel if they are not at fault, their response is to get angry, hurt, and or try to find who's at fault! When the same folk are the fault, they feel sad, guilty, and upset that they were caught.

The best response is to accept responsibility for the deed and try not to repeat the same thing! Acceptance puts you in a position to get past the condition, to learn from the error, and to free you from guilt and other negative responses. And with this freedom, you have the clarity to make a better choice later.

Taking full responsibility for the situation puts you in a position to make the necessary adjustments needed. This way there are no suppressed unresolved emotional feelings to cause unhealthy conditions in body, mind, or soul later.

NOTES

CHAPTER 20 - ATTACHMENT AND RELEASE

What is attachment? Bind by personalities. The state of being firmly attached to someone or something (as by affection, sympathy, or self-interest). What are you attached to? When you attach yourself to others, you won't know who is who, then freedom which love requires is bound and this will never do! Have you ever noticed that what you attach yourself to never lasts? Could it be that you've made a god of it and then Life shows you that these things are temporal and were not intended to be permanent? When we attach ourselves to another person we think we should feel what they feel and be in the exact space they are in. That's called co-dependent. Codependency doesn't work. As some of you know, it's a disease. There are very specific qualities that are portrayed. Think of two trees leaning against each other at the top; if one tree moves the other one falls and vice-versa. They tend to move as one unit instead of individuals. The pain in all this is that neither one is free to express themselves without the other. This is very limiting, even burdensome, and after a while, the relationship breaks. When you hold onto the other person so tightly you restrict them as well as yourself. There are many books and information on codependency, read Terry Cole-Whitaker's "What You Think of Me Is None of My Business". Total self-acceptance and unconditional love will help for starters; willing to trust yourself and take responsibility for your actions. When you are free, you are available Now!

To release something means that you are relieving yourself of the restraint or confinement of something. When you hold onto the past hurt, pain, and or emotions, it doesn't work! It's similar to holding onto a cactus; the tighter you hold it the more it hurts. Once released you can then remove the spines and the healing process can begin. The degree of intensity you hold onto the plant determines the effect of the physical, mental, and emotional damage to the body. These are the same effects the body experiences when it occurs with words, deeds, and or injury. So, to completely release it, heals.

Fortunately, or unfortunately, medication either masks the pain or covers it for some time. That's why it returns! It does not heal the condition. Therefore, the person gets some temporary relief. This is not to say don't take medication; that is your choice completely. I just want you to pay attention to how the body responds to it. Have you ever thought about this before; the first response to a minor physical pain (a slight bump of the knee); is to yell, then resist the pain by doing something to not have it. If the pain is experienced, consciously, for a moment it will disappear completely! So, to hold onto any pain causes you to re-experience it over and over.

To repress or suppress emotional pain is to have it build up over some time and cause suffering in body, mind, and soul. See the section on Methods of Pain Relief. You may have heard the adage of "mind over matter". Another method of release is to tell the truth in detail about the incident. When you talk to a therapist or friend about some trauma you've encountered it helps to relieve the emotional charge behind it. People holdonto pain because they are resisting it.

NOTES

CHAPTER 21 – METHODS OF PAIN RELIEF

Another method of release is to tell the truth in detail about the incident. When you talk to a therapist or friend about some trauma you've encountered it helps to relieve the emotional charge behind it. People hold onto pain because they are resisting it. Emotional pain sticks when it is held onto by the event as well. The more you talk about it, the less painful it becomes. Remember the emotional charge behind it goes away! You can always write this event in detail as well, and get the same results! Example: Let's say when you were in elementary school you were punished for being late back to class. Your punishment was to write something a hundred times. You wrote until your fingers got tired.

Now, in adult life, you don't like to write for any period! The anger, hurt, and disappointment you felt then show up now as resistance, making you feel that you just don't want to write at all! The solution is to process the event from back then and release yourself from its hold. Write the event in detail and forgive the teacher, yourself, and all the kids who laughed and made a joke out of it! Now you can come from real freedom of choice instead of automatic response!

NOTES

CHAPTER 22 - PHYSICAL BODY TEMPLE

1st Corinthians 3:16 says: Do you not know that you are the temple of God and that the Spirit of God dwells in you?

Your body is the living temple of God, the reason being that your body was constructed by A Life Force. You don't have to circulate your blood, digest your food, or make your eyes see or your ears hear. Something does that for you, even makes your heartbeat! So based on just that, taking care of your temple is a gift. You have a spiritual connection with this Life Force.

When you take care of your body properly it works for you. Knowing how to follow the messages your body gives you helps you to stay healthier and happier. Your intellect lets you become aware when something is not functioning right. And when you correct it, you're okay. Overdoing anything physically can cause concern. Overeating, overdrinking, overworking, etc., can cause the body to get devitalized quickly.

Think about it, when you overeat you don't feel as good as you would have if you hadn't! Consequently, under normal circumstances, you would feel satisfied and content. But you overdid it, and now are subject to having a stomachache or feeling bad one way or the other. And over long periods if you continue to overeat like this; you will end up being overweight and/or have different health conditions that you did not originally have. Now let's look at drinking, some people drink too much alcohol. Once they continue to over-drink alcohol the overage amount of it goes into the body and at some point, it will have the body call for the alcohol. This is known as alcoholism. Too much alcohol in the system causes all kinds of devitalization to the physical body temple. Not only does the person not realize what's happening in the body, but long periods of drinking cause the body to lose vital organs and systems to function improperly.

There are many many more reasons why not to drink too much alcohol! Some people think that overworking is a virtue and that it is honorable. And working too much can ruin the body Temple as well. It is okay to work, it is good to have a job. However, overdoing it does not help the physical body in the long run. Long periods of overworking cause problems too! Life seeks a balance, there's a time and place for everything! Can you even start to imagine how many things the workaholic misses out on that he is supposed to learn in this lifetime?

The life lessons and karmic debts he delays due to overworking. He misses out on all kinds of things that would help him to grow and to be happier and healthier.

NOTES

CHAPTER 23 - EXCUSES

Did you know that all the things you hold onto from the past block your good, now? Unresolved issues keep you stuck, unhappy, struggling, and filled with discontentment! So when someone is asking for information or confirmation, tell the truth at the moment or say nothing. Michael complains about his job and how things have changed since he started eleven years ago. The shifts, workloads, and ownership of the company have just changed. He was moved to the night shift and he hated it. And a lot of his longtime co-workers are now quitting because they didn't like the new changes either.

When I asked him what he was going to do he gave me a lot of excuses. He said "he has always been a loner, he's the type of person who is always early to work, he's put in extra hours to the company and the job. He makes sure that the job is done before he leaves. He has always respected the people in charge. He said that his dad told him he had to work hard and he has been this way all his life. That this must be his lot in life and that's the way it is". He continued on and on with one excuse after the other. Excuses keep him stuck unhappy and miserable! He doesn't know what he wants to do so he stays on this job complaining instead of admitting that he's afraid of change and scared to leave for another job somewhere else. Michael is holding onto old excuses and patterns that no longer serve him. He is still making excuses.

After weeks of complaining and being in this state of upset, he got sick. And now, with more excuses, his blood pressure is too high for him to go to another job and he won't pass the physical or make enough money. More excuses for three months, and then he finally admitted it was fear and that he was scared. It was hard for him to admit it, but he did. Then just two days later ideas for change popped into his head regularly! He started talking about new places to work and put in applications to other companies. And he had finally freed himself from some of his old lifetime excuses. When someone starts to justify reasons and excuses to stay the way they are and/or where they are now, they want to keep their old patterns. You have to allow it to be and pray that they eventually see the truth. And they might! And keep in mind that they have freedom of choice, just like you do! Michael will be getting a new job soon!

After growing through this for a while you may contend that "it's your lot in life" and become apathetic about it. Some may even say it's the family heritage they have. Others may say they're too young, too old, born with the wrong parents, the wrong era, too poor, the body type, wrong race, color, gender, and the list goes on! All this may appear reasonable, but it is not true. The truth is: is when we get involved with any kind of lie, falsehood, in any way, we suffer period. Lies don't work and they cause more problems than they're worthy and cause so many broken friendships and relationships prove it too.

Take for example: a so-called friendship for the person to gain camaraderie and connection to another person. Person # 1 may choose an outfit to wear to the dance. Her friend (so-called) person #2 is going to the dance too. Person, one asks person 2 if the outfit looks good. Person two thinks the outfit is inappropriate and ugly but doesn't say that instead of telling her the truth, her truth at the moment, she sugar-coats it and claims it looks okay. This may seem small and insignificant, yet it's the beginning of the end of the friendship! Untruths told for whatever reason don't work! As time goes by little sugar-coated lies continue to keep the relationship stuck.

Nothing can be built on lies anyway! Over some time, this relationship breaks because it never had an honest foundation in the first place! So, when someone is asking for info or confirmation tell the truth at the moment.

NOTES

CHAPTER 24 - LETTING GO OF THE PAST

Did you know that all the things you hold on to from the past block your Good Now? Unresolved issues keep you stuck, unhappy, struggling, and filled with discontentment. After growing through this for a while you may contend that "it's your lot in life" and become apathetic about it. Some may even say it's their family heritage. Others may say they're too young, too old, born with the wrong parents, the wrong era, too poor, wrong body type, wrong race, color, gender, and the list goes on! All this may appear reasonable, but it is not True! The truth is If we get involved in any kind of Lie (falsehood) in any way, we Suffer, Period! Lies don't work and they cause more problems than they're worth! There are so many broken relationships that prove this too.

For example, take a friendship between two people; Sally & Jane both are going to the school dance. Sally has chosen an outfit and asks Jane if it looks good. Jane thinks the outfit is ugly and inappropriate. Instead of telling Sally the truth (her truth) Jane sugar-coats it and claims it looks okay. This is the beginning of the end of that so-called friendship.
Untruths told for whatever reason don't work! Although this may seem harmless to the originator, it is enough to keep the friendship from growing on honest grounds. After some time, the constant little sugar-coats won't hold the relationship together. Sugar coats are distorted untruths, made-up! It causes the break-up because too many lies have caused it to be

on a shaky foundation. Hurt, disappointment, and upset follow! This is just one incident, think of the number of hours and years that go into a long-term relationship. Did you care for your friend at all? Sometimes these continuous, very small, incidents are enough to keep the relationship from renewal in the future.

NOTES

CHAPTER 25 - REGRETS

It's hard to try to live with regrets. They're usually things you'd like to forget. They consist of things that are always gone. Sometimes they're things you wish you had done! Regretting anything keeps you stuck in the past. It's like keeping something active and alive. You've already dealt with it, but you didn't want to let it go because you think there was something you wish you could have or should have done. And guess what? What's done is done! And to keep it alive in the present time only keeps you stuck with it! This is the situation: Ralph had a puppy Doberman pinscher dog, which he named Munch. This puppy was six months old. One day while Ralph was playing with the dog in the backyard his mother called him to come and eat lunch. He ran into the house and forgot to close the gate to the fence completely, and Munch ran out afterward. Ralph never saw the dog after that day. He started crying the next day after seeing that the dog was gone. He and his family looked for the dog. And they didn't find Munch anywhere that day.

Ralph's Dad worked the night shift and when he got home after midnight, he told Mom he had Munch in the back of his truck, and he wasn't alive. He told Mom that the dog must've been hit by a car and died. Now they had to figure out how to tell Ralph. The dad wanted to tell him the dog ran away and wouldn't be coming back and that he would buy him another one. The mom wanted to tell him the truth, the dog was dead and to bury the dog in the backyard. The truth works and after the Dad tells him what had happened, Ralph decides that he didn't want another dog. Ralph was 7 years old when Munch died and today, he is 35 and he has never owned or bought another dog!

NOTES

CHAPTER 26 - RENEWING THE MIND

Be ye transformed by the renewing of your mind. The only way to renew your mind is through your thinking! As a man thinks in his heart, so is he. So, whatever your thoughts are about yourself are the very experiences you will have. And when you agree with someone else's thoughts (esp. family) you'll have the same results from those thoughts too! There are thought patterns that we formed upon our growth from childhood; heard repeatedly, believed, and accepted as true, we operate from those very thought patterns today.

As grown-ups we can see their limitations and have the power to change these thoughts at any time in life we choose. We can even choose to keep them, though now we can see that they no longer serve us. Of course, the ones that are nice, pleasant, good, and of a good report can be kept. The ones we're speaking of are the ones that cause you pain, discomfort, upset, sickness, fear, limitation, and so forth. Have you heard the adage that says "thoughts are things"? Well, it's true. Everything is an idea before it becomes a manifestation. Thought is creative and has the power to objectify themselves.

The thoughts you think about your health determine the state your body is in. Sick thoughts make the physical body show the results. And healthy thoughts can heal the body. A person thinking healthy thoughts reflects the same in the body. I'm not saying that this or that condition is caused by thinking of that specific condition, but that the prolonged discordant mental state of mind will surely eventually become some physical ailment. Some people have died from great grief, of broken hearts; of outbursts of temper; of deep and continued resentment; of excessive worry, and many other mental states, in which there was no specific thought of sickness at all.

The main point to remember is that all mind activity inevitably tends to create its physical correspondence, so an unhealthy and morbid mental state projects itself into the physical body! Thought is the conscious activity of the one thinking and works as he directs, through Law; and this Law may be consciously set in motion! So, a realization of the Presence of God is the most powerful healing agency known to the mind of man.

NOTES

CHAPTER 27 - COMMUNICATION

Communication means: to make known and exchange of information or opinions, contiguous. Usually, conveyed by writing, speech, or signals. So, no wonder it's so important to communicate under all circumstances. In personal relationships, communication is one of the most important commodities. Without it, the relationship gets a death sentence. If there is a good open line of communication between the parties everything gets handled. This can easily be proven. Notice how communication becomes very natural and free flowing between two people: even if there's an argument.

There has to be a speaker and a listener. This exchange is necessary. Let's say, David and Carol, talk all the time planning, joking, laughing, or whatever. An incident happens to Carol, and she doesn't communicate it. This is a withhold. David tries to get her to share what has happened. She insists on not sharing the incident. He continues to try to communicate with her, but she keeps the withhold.

The free-flowing communication gets through with a short block attached. After a while, David will notice that he's not getting a response from Carol, and he will start to withhold too. The communication line is blocked and both parties have ceased to talk anymore. It's similar to feeling cut off when a loved one refuses to answer a question asked. Dead silence and lifelessness are felt. Communication is a part of sharing yourself with another person. The person who has the most withholds is the one who will want to leave the relationship first! To be able to share your deepest heartfelt feelings with another without fear of judgment, criticism, or loss is a wonderful experience! Most men are stuck with their unresolved issues, again, because of the façade and image they like to keep up!

Some may ask themselves, is it worth it? To chatter and talk about some things or topics just to hear yourself talk is not the same thing. Chit-chat is not real communication as communicating about yourself. Some like to appear unscathed by life's upsets, especially when dealing with others. This is an attitude that can be carried into adulthood. It appears as jargon or untruths about the speaker! The listener may not even pay attention to such talk.

NOTES

CHAPTER 28 - RESOLUTIONS TO RELATIONSHIPS

Relationships I feel don't work as well as they could because the individual who wants one does not ask themselves enough questions. To know what you want and why you want a relationship is important. What kind of relationship would you like; a long-term relationship, a hangout buddy, someone to just talk to, someone to take you to places when you have to have an escort, do you want a husband/wife, or do you want a live-in partner only? These are questions that you should ask yourself before you even go on a date.

The next thing that you need to do to get a good relationship is to ask what kinds of qualities and character traits the person has to have for you to be happy with them. Do they need to have money, do they need to be rich, do they need to be tall, or do they need to have a place to live in? You need to ask a lot of questions to find out and choose the right partner for you.

Then once you go to dinner or lunch you can talk to the person and find out in a very short period whether that person fits your picture for what you've chosen. Now remember what you see is what you get! It is very unlikely that that person will change to be what you want them to be. There are over 7.5 billion people on the planet, no one has to change who they are to be what you want them to be, and neither should you change to be how they want you to be. So, keep looking and notice the qualities early in the relationship.

Check to see if he has the qualities that are acceptable to you. If they are not you need to keep looking at all of their qualities. If the person has 95% of the qualities you want, this is acceptable to you. You might want to talk about the 5% that you don't see.

Now the communication lines have to open. You can make your agreement about anything that you both want and agree to. If he likes apples and you like oranges, he/ she may not want to eat them. And you should not have to not buy/eat oranges because he doesn't like them or not eat apples because you don't like them! That's a different arrangement. When the two of you come to an understanding and agreement about differences, talk it out!

NOTES

CHAPTER 29 - COMPLETING INCOMPLETE(S)

When you complete your incomplete(s) it keeps you clear and in the present time. You feel free and content. Think about it, if you finish something that you started you don't have to be concerned with yesterday, the past, or tomorrow, the future, you're done! Some people are so bogged down with incomplete(s) that they are tired and miserable before they get to work or wherever they are on their way.

Do you have something in your life that is incomplete? What about old unfinished projects you started a long time ago and didn't complete? Things like a book you started reading, an outfit you cut out and left undone, getting rid of old clothes in your closet, planting a new garden, writing a letter to someone, etc., etc., and so on. Having incomplete(s) around keeps you stuck. This too is a block for not getting what you want. Go through the incomplete(s) and complete them! You'll notice a big change in your life in many ways. It doesn't matter how you complete them, just get it done.

NOTES

CHAPTER 30 - THE PROCESS

These processes should be done when you are alone and have the time to complete them. Your time should not be interrupted. You should give yourself no less than 2 hours. The reason for this is most of the time there will be an emotional charge behind what you're recalling and you should feel free to allow yourself to completely express these feelings, undisturbed. When you are distracted by things happening in your surroundings, you will almost automatically resist the natural urge to let your feelings flow. This is one of the problems you're trying to eliminate; old, suppressed energy that has blocked you. So to deliberately be in a place where you're not free to release the blocks thoroughly won't help you.

When the process is done correctly there will be instant results! If it is done incorrectly, the results will not be there at all. Following the instructions precisely will eliminate any mistaken way of handling the issue you are working on. If you do the process at the time, you are emotionally upset, you will get instant results! The main thing to do is to write the issue down the way you have it set up in your experience. If you have a fear of dogs, that would be the way to set up your process sentence; all the reasons why I'm afraid of dogs are.

Example: Johnny has an anger issue with his younger brother, Tony. The issue was not only with his brother but with others in his life as well. One of the things to notice about yourself is that if you have an issue in one area of your life it's probably showing up in the other areas of your life also.

Remember the person who is afraid of dogs may have an issue of being afraid of other animals too. The dogs are the ones he can identify with the most, or there are dogs in the neighborhood now. It's not necessary to figure this part out as much as it is to work on the main one you are aware of now. Once you work on one main issue you will be handling some or all of the others in this area as well. So the first thing to do in the process is to see what issue you want to handle first. Each one should be handled individually.

The reason for this is because we have suppressed them one at a time; so, to dissolve them has to be the same way; one at a time! Once you start to process an issue your purpose is to get to the core or root of it. It's like an onion with its many layers; there's a thin one, a thick one, a film one, and so on. Or like a tree that has many branches off the trunk of it. Cutting the branches is like pruning it, it doesn't get to the root and uproot the tree and the branches always grow back! You intend to get to the core of your issue by processing it as completely as you can. The second step of the process is to write down the payoffs that you get by having or keeping the issue (condition).

A payoff is a secret reward or pleasure that you get by hanging onto the issue. It can be obvious or subtle. Example: When Maggie was a kid she didn't like bananas. She made a fuss and acted out, and her Grandma petted her and said she didn't have to eat them. So now in her adult life, she can refuse to eat bananas. The payoff for keeping this condition goes back to the petting, the attention, and the joy of having her way back then. Even now she can proudly say she doesn't like bananas! So, the payoff is something you get by keeping the issue!

The third step of the Process is to write down all the things you have to give up or let go of, to make things right. These are things you would have to let go of without judging or reasoning out. For instance, Maggie would have to be willing to let go of her resistance to bananas, she would have to give up her fear of getting sick, and so forth. See when Maggie was this little five-year-old kid who sneaked and ate four big bananas and had a terrible stomachache and from that moment she feared eating them again because she blamed the bananas for making her sick! And in essence, she got sick because she ate too many of them at one time! Over-eating was the cause. So, write down all the things you have to give up until they become repetitive, and then move to the next step.

The fourth step is to then write down your most negative thoughts about yourself! The Most Negative Thoughts about yourself will show up now. And whatever it is, The Eternal Truth is, always the exact opposite of the most negative thought! This should be written down as such too.

Your next and important step five is to tear up all the page(s) and throw them in the trash or you can burn them if there is a fireplace burning near you. The main thing is to tear them up as a symbol of you being done with this! **DO NOT KEEP THEM. DO NOT REREAD THEM AND DON'T SHARE ANY OF THEM WITH ANYONE!**

Below will be a list of the Process as it should be written, by you! If for any reason you are not clear about what to do, you might want to reread the samples above. You don't have to use any of the ideas from the samples; this is just to give you a little view of how to do the Process! Grammar, spelling, or a specific order is not necessary for this Process. If some thought or idea seems to be unrelated write it down anyway. Keep writing for all the thoughts that come into your mind at that moment. Some thoughts may have occurred when you were just a kid.

Kids don't always express themselves in a methodical order. So don't bother about the way your thoughts show up! You can use paper that you can write on front and back, scratch paper will do.

Remember you will be tearing it up and discarding it anyway! Again, there will be emotional charges behind doing your Process and you must be alone when you work! Remember there are no right or wrong answers. This is just your truth as you saw it.

NOTES

CHAPTER 31 - THE PROCESSES

1. Write down; All the reasons why I (have this condition, feel, think) or whatever the issue is. All the reasons why I don't like to write are…. My fingers get cramped after writing the same thing over and over again.

2. The payoffs I get by keeping this condition are I get to not write things I don't want to…I get to make up excuses…..

3. What I have to give up to make things right are…I have to let go of resistance…. I have to give up acting lazy…..

4. My most negative thought about myself is…Whatever the most negative thought about yourself at this point links to the final step number five.

5. The Eternal Truth Is….. ALWAYS the exact opposite of your most negative thought!

Draw the picture of the world and you inside and continue the dialogue.

This is your world. The big circle is the world. Somewhere in it, the dot; this is you and the circle around you is your little world. Included are the people, places, and things therein. When someone else or the people that come into your world reflect to you what you are having to work on or adjust within you, you may feel anger, hurt, upset, or many other emotions that you don't like. Any negativity that has risen in you, means you have work to do on yourself not the other person. It could have been anyone; relative, friend, stranger, etc. The problem is not them; it has risen in you. So start your process.

For example, Jack was doing fine. He appeared content and satisfied with himself. Then his old friend John showed up and he got angry. Now, John has pushed Jack off a swing when they were five years old. They are now adults and just the sight and sometimes the thought of John can cause Jack to be angry again. And so, Jack is the one with the problem he is no longer peaceful and content; he can't change John, he has to work on his issue. Let's say in a kitchen the stove is broken and you can work on the sink to doomsday, but the stove won't get fixed. So you are the one who responded the way you did when the person, place, or thing showed up.

NOTES

CHAPTER 32 - THE FORGIVENESS PROCESS

For this process, I suggest that you make a list of all the people that you need to forgive. Make another list of people who you feel need to forgive you! Then write them letters. It doesn't matter why you think you need to forgive them; you are following a Spiritual Law. You will not be sending the letter(s) to anyone, so grammar and spelling are not important! You must forgive someone for more reasons than you think. When you hold onto old hurts, pain, and upset from the past it causes you to get in trouble. Your money is blocked, your body suffers all kinds of conditions, and your joy is not there anymore.

Remember this: The past is gone, you can't change a minute, and the present is now, so bounce right back into it! We are told that it is a good thing to forgive people for all sorts of reasons. Jesus Christ forgave people who crucified him, so you really can forgive someone for his or her shortcomings! The main thing about the letter is to make sure you tell the person what they did, when they did it, and as much detail as you can come up with. Write out the incident completely (as much as you can recall) and tell them how you felt and how you were affected by it and anything else that seems pertinent to what happened. Then at the end of the letter you write "and for all these things I forgive you. ". Emotional charges WILL show up, so let these feelings flow and keep writing!

Don't make the mistake of forgiving the person without saying what they did. This doesn't work! Even if the person is no longer on the planet, you still have to forgive them! The letter is a way that you can resolve the issue before you see them again, or not. Someone asked, after forgiving the person do you have to interact with them again? The answer is not necessarily, the good part about this is that you are coming from true choice now instead of old outmoded past issues. You will make that decision without any problem. Your heart speaks for itself! When you write the letter asking for forgiveness for yourself, say whatever is there again, what you did and how you feel now, and that you are asking for their forgiveness.

At the end of this letter say, there is nothing between us but the Love of God! This is a big reminder; always write a forgiveness letter to yourself. For example: write, *I forgive myself for carrying anger, resentment, hurt, hatred, or whatever you have been carrying around. It can be a person, place, or thing.* Writing it is very, very important, and be sure to include as much detail as possible when writing. People find it easier to forgive others than themselves! God does not hold anything against you, neither does He withhold anything from you. You do that all by yourself.

The spiritual Laws have the punishment built right in them, so God doesn't have to punish you for not forgiving someone. Some people go for years without talking to their parents, and that doesn't work either.
You are supposed to Honor your mother and father, and what kind of honor can they get from you not resolving the issues that you have with them? Oh, you think that you are hurting them. Can, you be sure? Yes, they may be hurt for the time being, but your pain will last a whole lot longer!

They already have learned that there's nothing they can do if you don't want to cooperate. Then there's the generational handed-down pain to your kids (if you choose to have any).

The kids can inherit your bad attitudes and responses, just the way you did back then! There have been numerous cases where people became stuck with all that stuff they withheld from the past with their parents. A lot of them became ill and had health problems that they didn't have before their parents left the planet. So ask yourself, is it to your advantage to not forgive them for everything? Or to forgive everyone for everything! Think about it. Remember the real choice is always YOURS.

NOTES

CHAPTER 33 – SUMMARY

Clearing things up. You have read this far in the book and if you have used any of the processes in the book you are already feeling a shift in your mind and body. My purpose was to have you be aware of your issues that may be similar to or exactly like someone else's! And if you have patterns that are no longer serving you, you can work on them now rather than waiting for an incident to occur. Everyone picks up patterns from their environment as early as childhood. Some work and some do not. The patterns that are nice, pleasant, and of a good rapport should be kept.

Question your own actions and results day to day to see if you are satisfied. When you continue to work with the processes you'll get proof from your own experiences as to how you're doing. You get confirmation immediately. Keep in mind that you may have to write more than one forgiveness letter and do the process more than once. We suppress things like an onion, a thin layer, a thick one, a film, and so on until we reach the core! Also, do them often because you have had these patterns for a very long time. But once you clear them you will be healthy, happy, and content. Your life changes for the better whenever you work on you!

NOTES

ABOUT THE AUTHOR

Vera Key, a native of Atlanta, Georgia, is a professional nurse whose expertise extends beyond the realm of traditional medicine. A lifelong metaphysician, teacher, and counselor, Vera has shared her insights and wisdom through lectures and television appearances for many years. Her multifaceted interests include crafting natural soaps, cooking, sewing, and various forms of artistic expression.

Driven by a deep sense of compassion, Vera is committed to humanitarian work and has philanthropic endeavors planned for the future. She also looks forward to connecting with audiences through retreats and podcasts.

The inspiration for this book arose from Vera's interactions with countless individuals grappling with feelings of sadness, disappointment, and overwhelm. Witnessing their struggles, she felt compelled to offer guidance and support, particularly to those experiencing strained family relationships. Vera firmly believes that life encompasses far more than mere existence and dissatisfaction.

With this in mind, she embarked on a journey to empower individuals of all ages to cultivate healthier, happier, and more fulfilling lives. Vera's teachings have resonated with people from diverse backgrounds, and she remains dedicated to assisting those who seek to unlock their true potential and contribute meaningfully to the world.